SCRAWL!
Writing in Ancient Times

D0407125

SCRAWL!

Writing in Ancient Times

Prepared by Geography Department

Runestone Press ◆ Minneapolis

RUNESTONE PRESS · RUNESTONE

rune (rōon) *n* **1 a :** one of the earliest written alphabets used in northern Europe, dating back to A.D. 200; **b :** an alphabet character believed to have magic powers; **c :** a charm; **d :** an Old Norse or Finnish poem. **2 :** a poem or incantation of mysterious significance, often carved in stone.

Copyright © 1994 by Runestone Press,
a division of Lerner Publications Company

All rights reserved. International copyright secured. No part of this book may be reproduced or transmitted in any form or by any means, electronic or mechanical, including photocopying and recording, or by any information storage or retrieval system, without permission in writing from Lerner Publications Company, except for the inclusion of brief quotations in an acknowledged review.

Scrawl! Writing in Ancient Times is a fully revised and updated edition of *Ancient Scrolls,* a title previously published by Lerner Publications Company. The text is completely reset in 12/15 Albertus, and new photographs and captions have been added.

Thanks to Dr. Guy Gibbon, Department of Anthropology, University of Minnesota, for his help in preparing this book.

Words in **bold** type are listed in a glossary that starts on page 69.

Library of Congress Cataloging–in–Publication Data
  Scrawl! : writing in ancient times / prepared by Geography Department, Runestone Press.
    p. cm—(Buried Worlds)
  Includes index.
  ISBN 0-8225-3209-3 (lib. bdg.)
  1. Paleography—Juvenile literature. 2. Writing—Juvenile literature.
[1. Paleography. 2. Writing—History.]
I. Runestone Press. Geography Dept. II. Series.
Z107.S38 1994
411'.7—dc20   94–11980
                                                  CIP
                                                   AC

Manufactured in the United States of America
1   2   3   4   5   6   – I/JR –   99   98   97   96   95   94

411.7
SCR
1994

CONTENTS

WRITING IT DOWN

In the modern world, people depend on the written word to communicate with one another. They scan electronic messages and other data on computer screens. People read newspapers and magazines to learn about local and international events. Homeowners receive bills and business statements in the mail. But for most of the hundreds of thousands of years that humans have inhabited the earth, people have communicated by means other than writing.

The time period before people could write is known as **prehistory.** Although early humans did not leave behind written records, experts have been able to learn about prehistoric life from other kinds of information. From artifacts—such as bones, tools, and weapons—**archaeologists** (scientists who find and study ancient artifacts) have determined that prehistoric people were wanderers who hunted and gathered their food. They set up temporary camps by lakes and rivers or sought shelter in caves.

About 35,000 years ago, cave dwellers began painting pictures on the walls of their shelters. Using red, yellow, brown, and black colors, artists created images of bison, horses, and other animals. Many archaeologists believe that prehistoric hunters used these paintings to communicate with one another, but scholars have not determined exactly what kinds of information the cave artists were trying to relate. Words written with an alphabet usually have an agreed-upon meaning, but pictures hold different meanings for different people.

Prehistoric Cultures

Archaeologists identify any group that did not have a writing system as a prehistoric culture. The prehistoric period occurred at various times in different parts of the world. For example, in the A.D. 1500s—more than 4,500 years after the invention of the world's first writing system—European explorers discovered that the Aborigines of Australia had no writing system. Even today, some prehistoric cultures exist in remote areas of Africa and the Pacific Islands.

Prehistoric cultures created many ways to communicate without a written language. Most groups used memorization techniques to preserve historical knowledge. People memorized family histories, territorial contracts, and clan legends and passed this information from generation to generation. The Aborigines, for instance, have a long tradition of oral storytelling that continues in the present day.

Over time, many prehistoric cultures invented **mnemonics** (memory aids) to help keep track of important information. The earliest

This prehistoric painting of a horse is one of many pictures decorating the walls and ceiling of Lascaux Cave in France. Some archaeologists (scientists who dig up and study ancient objects) believe that early people created these images to communicate with one another.

mnemonics were stones marked with lines or dots, which probably helped people to count the passing days or the number of animals killed during a hunt. Some prehistoric cultures used message sticks. With this mnemonic, messengers carved notches on sticks to represent information dictated by clan leaders. At the time of delivery, the messengers followed the notches to help remember the important points of the message.

Many prehistoric cultures in the Americas developed mnemonics. Native American groups that lived in the northwestern region of North America, for example, crafted totem poles—wooden carvings that carried clan symbols.

Totem poles often told a family history or recorded a special event.

The Incas, who lived along the Pacific coast of South America, invented a memory aid called a quipu. Quipus consisted of several strings attached at intervals to one long string. To keep records, the Incas tied knots in the strings. The string's color, the way the knot was tied, and the knot's position each had a specific meaning. Sometimes a bunch of quipus were attached to another string called a summation cord, which totaled up all the information on the bunch.

Native American groups that lived along the Atlantic coast of North America used white and purple beads—called wampum—to

An Aborigine in Australia paints traditional geometric symbols on a tree branch. In ancient times, the Aborigines recorded signs on sticks to remember the important details of messages.

An artist on the South Pacific island of Tahiti chisels a totem pole. Many ancient cultures, especially those in Africa and in the Americas, carved symbols on totem poles to display family emblems or to record important events in a clan's history.

record treaties. Artisans made small holes in the beads and strung them onto belts. The beaded designs were usually geometric symbols, each of which represented a different term in a treaty. A sachem, or member of the clan council, was responsible for knowing the treaty and used the belt as a memory aid.

The Invention of Writing

Over a long period, hunters and gatherers became farmers and skilled craftspeople. Many people stopped wandering from place to place and began to set up permanent villages. Eventually, these early settlers needed ways to keep track of crop volumes, inventories, and trade. Although many mnemonics dealt with tallying and record keeping, they did not show what kinds of objects were being counted. To record information about specific items, people drew **pictographs**—the earliest stage of a writing system.

The first pictographs were simple. An ox head, for example, stood for one ox. Three ox heads

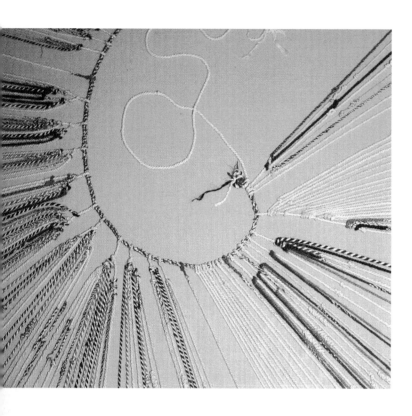

The Incas of South America kept records on quipus *(left)*, or groups of knotted strings. Each knot held a different meaning based on the way it was tied and on the color of string used. To record treaties and other important events, some Indian groups in North America strung geometric patterns of white and purple beads called wampum onto belts *(below)*.

represented three oxen. Gradually, pictures began not only to symbolize objects but also ideas. Such images are called **ideograms.** For instance, a picture of a mouth might also come to mean "speak." Other ideograms involved combining two or more images to represent one idea. A picture of a mouth and of food together, for example, probably stood for "eat."

A major step in the development of writing took place when people started using signs—called **logographs**—to represent individual words in their languages. Recorders might have drawn a crown to represent the word *king.* Or a spear may have been the sign for "to kill." To write the sentence "The king killed a deer," a recorder would draw a crown, a spear, and

Painted on bark by prehistoric Aborigines, this pictograph shows a hunter spearing a kangaroo.

a deer. Instead of drawing a complete picture of the king throwing a spear at a deer, the recorder used a symbol for each word.

Eventually, people began to use a syllabic system, in which the sign for a word could be used not only for that word but also for parts—or syllables—of other words. This stage is called **rebus writing.** In a modern example of rebus writing, images of a bee and of a leaf could be combined to make the word *belief.*

Soon people began to make simple symbols to stand for different sounds in their languages. When a community of people agreed on which sounds these signs represented, the symbols were considered an **alphabet.** For example, each of the 26 letters of the Roman alphabet—which is used for many languages, including English—has at least one agreed-upon sound. Different letters are usually combined to stand for the various sounds of a spoken language.

Symbol in use about 3100 B.C.	Symbol in use about 2500 B.C.	Symbol in use about 1800 B.C.	Symbol in use about 600 B.C.	SUMERIAN WORD (translation)
	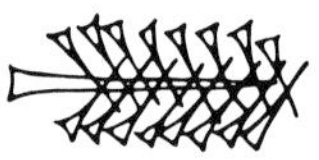			SE (grain)
				KUB (mountain)
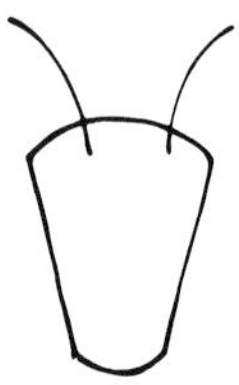	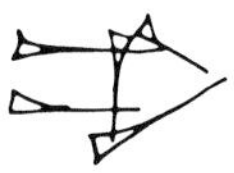	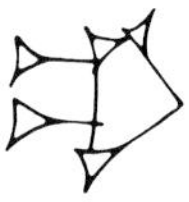	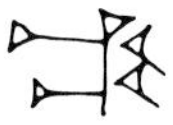	GUD (ox)

This chart shows the evolution of the cuneiform writing system, which was invented by the Sumerians of ancient Mesopotamia (modern Iraq). The earliest characters were pictographs (far left). By 2500 B.C., the Sumerians were using wedge-shaped writing (middle rows), which gradually changed until each symbol represented a sound (far right).

Archaeologists have discovered hundreds of well-preserved cuneiform tablets at sites throughout Mesopotamia. Priests in Sumerian cities used cuneiform writing to keep track of inventories and other economic information.

The First Writers

Archaeologists believe that the first people to invent writing were the Sumerians, who lived in southern Mesopotamia (modern Iraq) from about 4000 B.C. to 2300 B.C. The Sumerians—who were skilled farmers, craftspeople, and traders—built the world's earliest cities. From large temples within Sumerian cities, priests controlled trade. To help track inventories, the priests first developed pictographs, which later evolved into a writing system called **cuneiform.**

The ancient Egyptians adorned their temples and stone monuments with hieroglyphics, a writing system made up of picture-symbols. Used mainly for religious purposes, Egyptian hieroglyphics included more than 700 characters.

The Egyptians, who lived in northeastern Africa, probably got the idea for writing from the Sumerians. Archaeological evidence shows that the two civilizations had contact with one another. The Egyptians invented their own picture-writing system called **hieroglyphics.** The Sumerians also spread the idea for writing to the Indus civilization, which arose in what are now Pakistan and India. Archaeologists have found only a few traces of Indus writing, however, and know very little about it.

The notion of a writing system eventually spread northward to Crete, a Greek island in the Mediterranean Sea. From the eighteenth to the fifteenth centuries B.C., the inhabitants of Crete used a script called Linear A. In the fifteenth century B.C., the Mycenaeans of Greece overran Crete and adapted Linear A into a new writing system called Linear B.

About 1500 B.C., the Chinese, who lived far east of the Sumerians in what is now China, invented their own writing system. The Chinese used logographs, which at first were detailed pictures and later became symbols that represented whole words. The Chinese writing system never developed into an alphabet and remains

The inhabitants of the Greek island of Crete recorded information with Linear B, a writing system whose characters represented sounds.

much the same today as it was in 200 B.C. Modern Chinese writing now consists of more than 50,000 logographs.

On the other side of the world, the Maya independently invented a writing system sometime after A.D. 250. The Maya lived in Meso-america, a region that includes the modern countries of Mexico, Guatemala, Belize, Honduras, and El Salvador. The people of this ancient

Like the ancient inhabitants of China, present-day Chinese writers use a system of logographs—pictures that represent words. This modern logograph stands for the word forest.

15

civilization made elaborate pictographs and ideograms. Archaeologists call this writing hieroglyphics, although it does not look like Egyptian writing. Recent studies of the Mayan writing system have revealed that it contains some syllabic elements. But further examination is needed to fully decode this script.

A cloth rubbing from a stela (a pillar that commemorates a person or special event) reveals hieroglyphic writings. These writings belong to the Maya of Mesoamerica, a region that includes the modern countries of Mexico, Honduras, Belize, Guatemala, and El Salvador. Recent studies suggest that some Mayan hieroglyphics may have stood for sounds.

Sequoyah invented an 85-character alphabet for the Cherokee language.

SEQUOYAH'S SYSTEM

During the early 1800s, the Cherokee Indians, who lived mainly in and around North Carolina, were prosperous hunters, farmers, and traders. They had formed a government called the Cherokee Nation. The Cherokee did not have their own written language, however, and many clan members were unfamiliar with written English, a language brought to America from England by white settlers.

Sequoyah, a Cherokee respected for his knowledge of his people's traditions and religion, believed that a Cherokee writing system would improve the quality of life for the Cherokee clan. In 1821, after 12 years of work, Sequoyah completed a set of 85 symbols that represented every sound in the Cherokee language. He borrowed some letters from the English writing system and invented others.

Within months, thousands of Cherokee had learned to read and write Sequoyah's alphabet. His invention enabled his people to make written records of their history and culture and to publish books and newspapers for the Cherokee Nation.

WRITING MATERIALS

Archaeologists have discovered many different kinds of ancient writings, including burial inscriptions, trading records, legal documents, religious works, and private letters. The surfaces that early people wrote on also varied, usually according to the materials commonly found in their region.

Clay, Stone, and Metal

In Mesopotamia clay was abundant on the banks of the Tigris and the Euphrates rivers. The Sumerians shaped wet clay into tablets and wrote on them while the clay was still soft. When the writing was completed, the tablet was baked in an oven until the clay became dry and hard.

Sumerian clay tablets often consisted of two parts—an inner core on which a message was written and an outer layer of clay that covered the core and displayed the same message. To read the tablet, people usually consulted only the outer layer. But if the tablet was damaged, the outer layer could be broken and the original record beneath it could be read.

Because hardened clay does not decay, many Sumerian tablets remain in excellent condition. People in other regions also used clay as a writing material. Archaeologists have learned a great deal from the well-preserved tablets found throughout the world.

Stone was also a lasting material, and many important records and inscriptions were preserved in this hard substance. Recorders usually

Made from clay, an inner tablet and its outer envelope display duplicate messages. The ancient Sumerians invented this technique to ensure that at least one intact copy of a communication reached its destination.

ALBUQUERQUE ACADEMY
LIBRARY

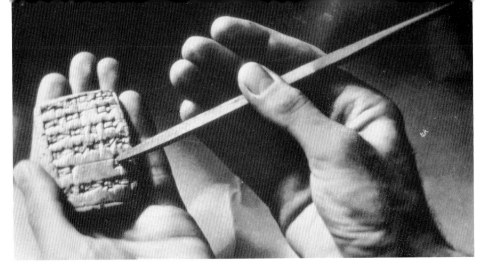

The Sumerians pressed the wedge-shaped characters of their cuneiform writing system into wet clay (above), and baked the tablet until it hardened. Unlike baked clay, which can break but does not decay, the copper metal of this ancient scroll (below) has corroded.

cut signs into a stone surface with a hammer and chisel. Like modern people, most ancient chiselers were right-handed. As a result, the blow of the hammer was usually delivered from right to left, making it easiest to carve the signs in that direction. This technique led to the development of some written languages that were read from right to left.

Writing on stone was a painstaking process. For this reason, most ancient civilizations reserved stone-carving for important monuments and significant religious works.

Very few ancient metal documents exist. Metals, such as gold and copper, had to be melted down and molded into sheets for writing. Because the metalworking process took time and because metal resources were scarce in some areas, metal was probably used less often than clay or stone.

Carved in stone—the most durable writing material of ancient times—the Greek inscription on this tablet has withstood hundreds of years of wear.

In addition, people were much more likely to melt metal for making tools, weapons, and money than for making writing material. But many writers chose metal for its beauty and durability, and some examples have survived to modern times.

Wood and Wax

Inscribing messages on stone or metal was slow and difficult. Moreover, these materials could take up a lot of space. To be more efficient, ancient people often wrote on softer and lighter materials,

The ancient Greeks and Romans posted important public notices on wooden boards called albums, which could be painted to make way for new messages.

such as wood, wax, and small pieces of pottery.

When wood is exposed to damp conditions, it quickly rots. So most of the wooden tablets that have survived to the present day were preserved in dry places, such as in the desert. The early Chinese collected entire libraries made up of writings on bamboo and palm wood. The Greeks and Romans—who lived on the northwestern coast of the Mediterranean Sea—did not use many wooden tablets, but officials did display important public notices on whitened boards

In Asia, some ancient writers wrote on palm wood and folded the material into accordion-shaped books.

THE ART OF ARABIC

Arabic is the official language of many Arab nations in the Middle East and North Africa. People in these regions may speak Arabic in different dialects (variations of vocabulary and pronunciation), but the written language is the same throughout the Arab world.

The Arabic alphabet has 28 characters, each of which stands for a sound. Written from right to left or from top to bottom, Arabic is a cursive script that is geared for rapid penwork. Writing this alphabet is also an important art form. Many Arab artists carefully inscribe the flowing Arabic sym-bols within intricate, multi-colored geometric designs.

Experts are uncertain when Arabic originally developed, but they do know that the inhabitants of the Arabian Peninsula were the first to use it. Arabic is the alphabet used in the Koran, the sacred writings of the Islamic religion. Islam began on the Arabian Peninsula, and as the religion's following spread to neighboring lands, so did the Arabic alphabet. In recent times, Arabic has become an important language in international business and politics.

Surrounded by an ornate border, this example of Arabic writing is from a sixteenth-century Koran. The Koran contains writings that are sacred to Muslims.

called albums. These boards were whitewashed again and again to cover and replace the old notices with new messages.

A wax tablet—shaped like a shallow, rectangular cooking pan—consisted of a wooden base with raised edges that held a sheet of wax. The wood gave the tablet strength and firmness, and the wax provided a smooth, soft surface that was easy to inscribe.

Ancient people wrote on wax tablets with a special tool called a

The early Romans, who used wax as a common writing surface, sometimes joined the tablets together at the left edge to make a codex, the forerunner to the world's first books.

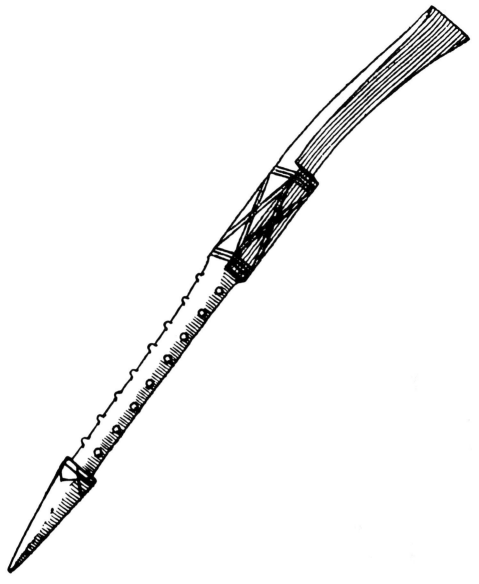

Ancient recorders wrote on wax tablets with a stylus, a sharp, pointed writing tool. The flat end of the stylus could be used to smooth out mistakes.

stylus. One end of this instrument was sharply pointed for writing. To erase a wax tablet, writers smoothed out the surface with the other end of the stylus, which was broad and flat. Because wax tablets were so easy to erase, they were one of the most convenient writing materials in ancient times.

Temporary writings, such as public announcements, were often scratched onto wax tablets. Sometimes even legal and financial records were kept on this material. At Pompeii, an ancient Roman seaport in what is now Italy, archaeologists found contracts for loans and other banking records

A potter on the Mediterranean island of Cyprus uses traditional methods to shape a clay pot. In ancient times, the large, flat pieces of broken pottery provided excellent writing surfaces.

written on wax. Once the loans had been paid or the transactions were concluded, the contracts were no longer needed and could be erased.

Writers sometimes fastened wax tablets together with a ring so that they could be turned like the pages of a book. This grouping of tablets was called a **codex,** a word that also refers to a writing composed of many sheets.

Ostraca

Potsherds—pieces of broken pottery—were another convenient

writing material. Ancient potters shaped a wide variety of household and decorative vessels from clay and baked the items to make them permanently hard. Pottery often broke, however, and ancient people wrote on the potsherds in the same way that modern people might use scrap paper.

Archaeologists refer to potsherds that carry inscriptions as **ostraca.** This name comes from the potsherd voting ballots used in Athens, a city-state in ancient Greece. An Athenian council sometimes held secret votes to decide if someone was too dangerous to live in the city. The ballots were written on

Bowls and other household wares often broke, leaving behind an unlimited supply of potsherds. Pieces of pottery that bear writing are called ostraca.

This ostracon bears Egyptian hieroglyphics. Ancient writers either scratched characters into the hardened clay or wrote on the smooth surface with paint or ink.

ostraca and placed in a pot. Anyone who received too many negative votes was ostracized and banished from Athens for 10 years.

Although ostraca were meant to be temporary, they proved to be almost indestructible. Excavators have found thousands of ostraca throughout the world, and they have provided much useful information about ancient life. In Egypt, for example, people once used ostraca as tax records. After workers paid their taxes each year, they threw away their receipts. From the discarded ostraca, archaeologists have learned a great deal about the Egyptian tax system.

THE INDIC ALPHABETS

After the Roman and Arabic alphabets, the Indic is the most widely used system in the world. People in India and in many other Asian nations east of India write with some type of Indic alphabet. Although the residents of these areas speak different languages, the Indic writing systems they use all come from Brahmi, the earliest Indic alphabet.

Some experts believe Brahmi, which developed between the eighth and the sixth centuries B.C., has its roots in a script used in the ancient Indus Valley (modern Pakistan and northwestern India). Other scholars think Brahmi is a variation of Aramaic, a writing system that may have been brought to India by sea traders from ancient Mesopotamia (present-day Iraq).

The Brahmi alphabet eventually branched into two types. North Indic alphabets have characters with straight lines because the letters were originally carved in wood. South Indic alphabets, on the other hand, feature curved lines. These signs were first recorded on palm leaves, which would have slit if a writer used straight strokes.

Over the centuries, traders, adventurers, and religious groups spread the Brahmi alphabet from India to other cultures, each of which adapted the system to its own spoken language. In modern times, more than 25 different Indic alphabets are in use.

These characters are written in the Devanagari script, an Indic alphabet used mainly in India.

PAPYRUS, PARCHMENT, AND PAPER

Tablets made of stone, clay, wax, and wood were effective writing surfaces, but they were still heavy and bulky. When ancient people wanted to write down dozens of songs, to inventory thousands of items in a palace storeroom, or to record the history of an important conquest, they needed many of these unwieldy tablets.

A large number of heavy tablets was hard to carry from place to place and needed a lot of room for storage. To solve this problem, ancient people developed lighter and more compact writing materials.

Papyrus

In ancient Egypt, a tall marsh plant called **papyrus** grew in the fertile land along the Nile River. From this plant, the Egyptians made a variety of products, such as food, medicine, clothes, rugs, sails, ropes, and chewing gum. The papyrus plant was so important to the Egyptians that they used it as an official national symbol.

The stem of the papyrus plant was also used to make the world's first light, compact writing material. When pressed into thin, flat sheets, papyrus resembled paper.

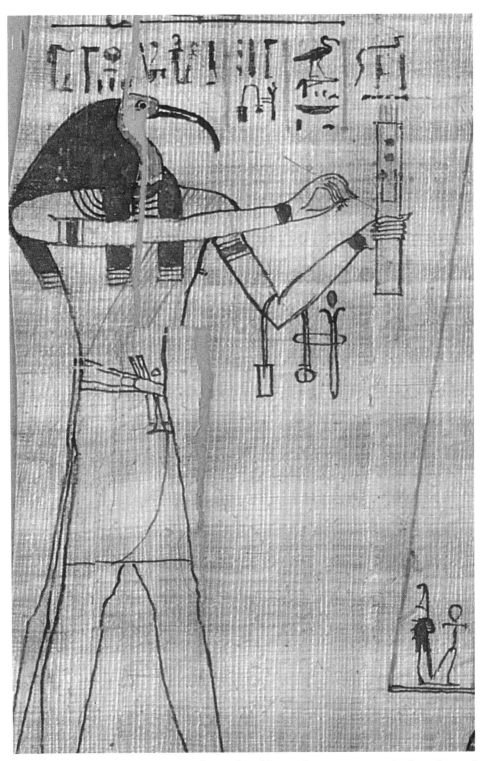

This section of an Egyptian text from the thirteenth century B.C. depicts the god Thoth holding the tools of an ancient writer. The fragment clearly shows the texture of papyrus, a writing material made from the stem of the papyrus plant.

In fact, the name "paper" comes from the word *papyrus*.

To prepare papyrus for writing, workers removed the outer bark from the lower part of the plant's thick stem. The spongy material inside the stem was then peeled off in strips, which were flattened to form sheets. A second layer of strips was placed on top of the first one, with the strips running at right angles to the first layer. Workers then beat the papyrus with a hammer until the two layers had fused into a single sheet. The result was a strong, flat writing surface with vertical lines on one side and horizontal lines on the other. After the papyrus sheet dried, it was cut to a standard size and smoothed with a light, powdery stone called pumice.

The Egyptians used single sheets of papyrus for letters or notes. Writers attached the ends of many sheets together to make a **scroll** (a long roll) for lengthy manuscripts. Most scrolls consisted of about 20 sheets, each of which was 16 to 18 inches (41 to 46 centimeters) long. But some were as long as 133 feet (40.5 meters)—almost half the length of a football field.

The Egyptians also used enormous amounts of papyrus for records and documents. Although the papyrus plant grew in abundance, the time and effort put into

Each finished sheet of papyrus consisted of two layers. Long, thin strips from the papyrus plant's stem were flattened and placed at right angles to one another. With hammers, workers pounded the strips until they fused into a single sheet.

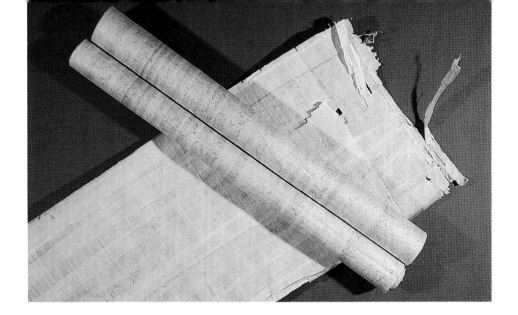

making each sheet of papyrus made the material expensive. For this reason, papyrus scrolls were often scrubbed clean and used again and again. This practice was especially common in schools, where students needed a lot of blank sheets.

Papyrus became very popular throughout the Mediterranean and the Middle Eastern regions. Egypt exported large quantities of this effective writing material and dominated the market for nearly 4,000 years.

In ancient times, the papyrus plant (right) grew in abundance in the Nile River's marshes and provided a huge supply of writing material (above). Overharvesting eventually made the plant scarce.

An Egyptian tomb painting from about 1450 B.C. portrays workers harvesting papyrus.

Writing on Papyrus

The Egyptians wrote on papyrus with a soft reed brush that had to be repeatedly dipped in ink, which was made from a mixture of soot, water, and sticky sap. The Greeks improved on this system by using only hard reeds, whose tips could be split in two to form a cavity that held ink. The ink was very durable, and some ancient papyrus scrolls can still be read without difficulty.

After scrolls were completed, they were kept safe in many ways. Librarians tagged some scrolls with identification labels and placed the rolls on open shelves. People also stored scrolls in baskets and jars. Other scrolls were stored in special boxes, each of which held 10 rolls. This storage method has posed difficulties for archaeologists who have found that entire boxes of scrolls were lost. As a result, some lengthy ancient writings are missing large sections of text.

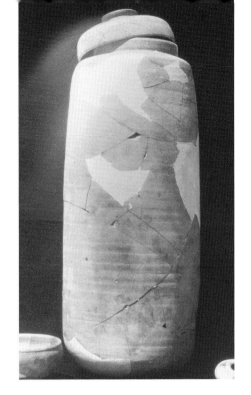

Ancient writers stored papyrus scrolls in many ways. For example, tall jars (right) *helped keep documents dry, while tagged scrolls stored on shelves* (below) *could be easily identified.*

Surviving Papyrus Scrolls

Although most of the countries that border the Mediterranean Sea are warm and dry much of the year, the winter often brings rain. In damp weather, papyrus manuscripts quickly decay. For this reason, few papyrus manuscripts have survived compared to the many that archaeologists believe once existed.

In Europe the largest collection of papyrus scrolls comes from Herculaneum, a Roman city on the Italian Peninsula. The eruption of the volcano Mount Vesuvius destroyed Herculaneum in A.D. 79. An entire library of papyrus scrolls, buried for many centuries beneath a thick layer of volcanic ash, miraculously survived.

Outside of Europe, the largest number of ancient papyrus scrolls has been found in Egypt, where the dry desert climate beyond the Nile River Valley preserved perishable materials, such as wood and papyrus. Over many centuries, some parts of the Nile Valley dried up as well. Areas that had once been fertile farmland turned into deserts, and the towns in those areas were abandoned.

In the ruins of these towns, archaeologists have found large numbers of papyrus writings, including some important literary works. Most of these writings were the work of Greek authors who traveled to Egyptian lands and strongly influenced the Egyptian culture. Workers have **excavated** (dug up) numerous texts by the famous Greek poet Homer, as well as dozens of plays by ancient dramatists.

Archaeologists have discovered many well-preserved Egyptian papyrus fragments, such as this illustration from the tenth century B.C.

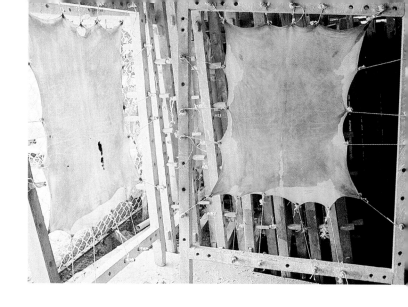

Stretched across wooden frames, animal skins (right) stand ready to be finished into parchment. Parchment provided a smooth writing surface on which writers and illustrators could more easily apply intricate designs (below).

During the second century B.C., the Roman Empire encompassed widespread colonies and administrative centers. The empire's rapid growth contributed to a high demand for papyrus. Papyrus was becoming increasingly scarce, and the price of the material rose. As a result, ancient people began looking for another writing surface that was equally light, smooth, and convenient.

Parchment

Ancient people gradually came to depend on **parchment,** a writing material made from the skins of certain animals. Parchment was

37

After washing and stretching animal skins, a parchment maker scrapes the material to make it thinner.

first used about 4,000 years ago when papyrus was plentiful. As the centuries passed and the supply of papyrus declined, the use of parchment increased. By about A.D. 500, parchment had replaced papyrus as the most common writing material. Parchment remained the principal writing material of Europe and the Middle East until the Chinese invention of paper spread westward in the eighth century A.D.

To make parchment, the skins of cattle, sheep, or goats were soaked in water, cleaned of all flesh and hair, and smoothed carefully. At this point, the skins were stretched tight and left to dry. The skins of calves and kids were used to make a particularly fine grade of parchment called **vellum.** With both types of parchment, the result was a hard, flexible sheet that had the consistency of a piece of thin, strong cardboard. The parchment sheet was then rubbed with chalk and pumice to make it smooth and white. After trimming off the irregular edges and cutting it into sheets, the parchment was ready for writing.

While ancient people mainly used papyrus for temporary administrative records, parchment was a common material for some permanent writings. Works of literary or religious importance had to be inscribed on a durable material, and writers turned to parchment for this purpose. In modern times, people continue to use parchment for important documents, such as diplomas and legal papers.

Writing on Parchment

Writers inscribed texts on parchment scrolls in one or more columns from top to bottom. Before writing, however, recorders marked out vertical lines that indicated the margins of each column. Then, within these vertical margins, writers measured the number of horizontal lines that would fit within each column, leaving wide margins at the top and at the bottom. These horizontal lines were lightly scored (scratched) into the surface with a sharp knife and can still be seen on some ancient scrolls.

As a writing material, parchment differed from papyrus in some important ways. Parchment was more durable and could withstand more wear and tear. Unlike papyrus scrolls, which wore out easily and had to be frequently recopied, parchment scrolls lasted for a long time. A disadvantage of parchment—especially during its early years—was that the outer, or hair, side of the skin was a different color and texture from the inner, or flesh, side. The flesh side was naturally smoother, and until parchment's manufacture was improved, only this side was good enough to use for writing.

From Scrolls to Books

Writers initially sewed individual sheets of parchment together to look like papyrus scrolls. Although scrolls, when unrolled, were easy to read from beginning to end, they had certain drawbacks. To look up information in a document, for example, ancient people had to roll and unroll the scroll to the appropriate places. This was time-consuming with a long scroll and created a great deal of wear and tear on the material.

Unlike papyrus, which often cracked when folded, parchment could bend without breaking. Ancient people discovered that by folding parchment into more manageable, paged sections—the design of which was based on the wax tablet codex—information was easier to find.

To make a book, parchment sheets were cut to a standard size and collected into groups of four sheets. Bookmakers folded the sheets into sixteen pages—called quires—and poked tiny holes through the sheets to map out a measuring grid for uniform margins and column widths on each page. The sheets were then unfolded and ready for inscription. When the text was completed, the bookmakers refolded the sheets. Many quires were sewn together at the left edge to make a book.

The Invention of Paper

Papyrus and parchment were forerunners of the modern writer's most common material—paper.

A papermaker dips a mesh mold filled with pulp into a vat of water while other workers dry and flatten finished sheets.

A manuscript made by the Aztecs of Mesoamerica in the A.D. 1500s shows the property records of a Mexican village. The inhabitants of Mesoamerica invented a type of paper made from tree bark.

The Chinese produced the first paper as early as the third century B.C. Archaeologists have unearthed examples of very coarse, yellowish paper that came from the inner bark of the mulberry tree. Chinese papermakers collected fibers from the bark, mixed them with water, and pressed the material into a shallow mesh-covered mold. When the water drained through the mesh, the molded fibers resulted in a thin sheet of paper. The Chinese later experimented with other fibrous materials for making paper, such as rags, cork, and fishnets.

For 600 years, papermaking techniques were known only in

A machine forms pulp into a wet sheet of paper. Modern technology allows factories to manufacture large quantities of paper quickly.

China and in a few neighboring lands. The Chinese carefully guarded their methods and profited greatly from the export of paper to settlements in the Middle East and in the Mediterranean. Papermaking spread to other areas of the world in the eighth century A.D., after two Chinese paper producers were imprisoned and forced to reveal the process to an Arabian governor. The Arabs, who lived on the Arabian Peninsula and in other parts of western Asia, had long imported paper from China.

By 795 a paper industry was well-established in Baghdad, a city in what is now Iraq. From there, papermaking spread to Europe, where the first mills used water-driven machines to produce paper. Paper made from trees was faster and cheaper to manufacture than any earlier writing material and helped to make paper products, such as books, more accessible to the general population.

The Maya of Mesoamerica also made an early type of paper. Workers collected and pounded the inner bark of wild fig trees until the bark strips reached the consistency of cloth. The material was then covered with a thin layer of lime, a mineral substance that hardened the writing surface. This paperlike material was usually folded like an accordion to make a book.

Although modern papermaking methods take advantage of advanced machinery for large-scale manufacturing, the basic techniques are the same as they were in ancient times. And paper continues to be the world's most popular writing material.

READING THE ROSETTA STONE

For hundreds of years, scholars struggled to understand the hieroglyphic writings of ancient Egypt. A breakthrough finally came in 1799. In that year, a Frenchman found a tablet half buried in mud near the Egyptian city of Rosetta. Known as the Rosetta stone, this tablet contains a royal decree written in three languages.

The first inscription is in ancient hieroglyphics. The second is in Demotic, a script used in Egypt during the third century B.C. The same message appears at the bottom of the stone in classical Greek—a script long known to experts.

Using the Greek text as a guide, the French scholar Jean Francois Champollion was able to decode the ancient Egyptian hieroglyphics. Champollion's thorough study of the Rosetta stone was an important key to understanding the ancient Egyptian civilization and has helped language experts to read many other ancient texts.

The Rosetta stone, which provided the key to understanding ancient Egyptian hieroglyphics, is almost 4 feet (1.2 meters) high, 2.5 feet (.76 m) wide, and 11 inches (28 centimeters) thick.

THE SCRIBES

In ancient times, very few people could read or write. The individuals who possessed these skills were usually highly educated professional writers called scribes. People in cities, as well as in small communities, relied on scribes to write business contracts, legal documents, and many other vital materials. For this reason, scribes held important—and often powerful—positions in many ancient societies.

The Schooling of a Scribe

From ancient writings, archaeologists know a great deal about the education of scribes in Mesopotamia and Egypt, where scribal schools had been established by about 3000 B.C. Students attended classes from dawn until late

afternoon for all but a few days of every month. They began school at age 6 and continued their studies until they became full-fledged scribes at about age 18. In both societies, this education was often administered by religious officials, and many schools were attached to temples.

The students focused almost their entire educational career on the art of writing. Under the guidance of a head teacher and a staff of assistants, students memorized hundreds of complicated signs. Egyptian hieroglyphics contained more than 700 symbols, and the list of Mesopotamian cuneiform characters was no shorter. Young scribes spent hours copying and recopying these marks until they had perfected each symbol. To practice their writing skills, students

This painted sculpture from about 2500 B.C., depicts a young Egyptian scribe. In ancient Egypt, students trained for 12 or more years to become scribes.

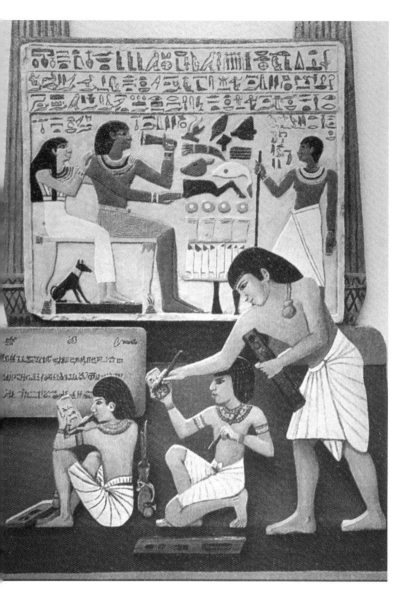

An Egyptian instructor teaches a pupil how to write hieroglyphics.

duplicated lists of words and wrote their own essays and poems.

Some teachers were specialists who taught students how to draw up legal contracts or instructed classes in the technical terms used by healers, priests, judges, and merchants. Studies also included a wide variety of subjects, including music and art. Mathematics, another important aspect of a scribe's education, eventually enabled students to compute the interest payments on loans or to figure out how much grain a farmer needed to sow a field of specific dimensions.

To graduate from a scribal school, students had to prove that they possessed the proper skills. Through lengthy oral and written examinations a panel of master scribes judged each pupil on all the subjects taught during the pupil's training. Students who passed the rigorous tests became scribes and worked at a wide variety of jobs.

In small communities, for example, scribes often read and wrote letters for citizens. Some skilled writers found jobs administering large estates or drawing up contracts for merchants. Courts needed scribes to read and record evidence in legal cases. Other writing experts became temple administrators or ambassadors. The most skilled

An Egyptian scribe's writing case held a reed pen and a water jar. A picture-symbol of this case became the Egyptian hieroglyphic character for scribe.

scribes held influential positions, assisting government officials or even kings.

The Copiers

As time passed, more and more people learned to read and write, and they wanted their own copies of important manuscripts. Some merchants, called stationers—who were much like modern book-sellers—worked as brokers for customers and scribes. A customer told the stationer the style and price range of a needed manuscript, and the merchant found a scribal

Records from several areas of the world show that in ancient times many women could write, and some women were trained as scribes. Beginning in the ninth century A.D., women of the Japanese aristocracy learned to write in hiragana, a script that uses symbols to represent sounds.

A Hebrew scribe copies passages from a completed scroll. Workers employed many ancient scribes as copyists, and large groups of copyists often collaborated to duplicate lengthy documents.

workshop that would complete the project.

Some scribes functioned only as copiers. They would either work alone, duplicating an original document, or they would write down what another scribe read aloud. Although these methods of copying were fairly effective, they sometimes resulted in errors that could change the meaning of the text.

If a manuscript was copied by sight, for example, a careless scribe might omit entire lines or paragraphs or even repeat a whole passage. If a scribe recorded a manuscript that was read aloud, two words that sounded alike might become confused. The incorrect word would be written in place of the one that was intended. In ancient times, specialists known as correctors were employed to fix as many of these mistakes as possible.

To fix an error, a corrector might have scraped or wiped off the old ink and written in the intended word or passage. Or the writer simply might have crossed out the error and written in the correction. The latter method has provided paleographers—modern scholars of ancient writings—the opportunity to read both versions and to decide which one is more likely to be accurate.

Hebrew scholars known as Massoretes copied and amended this page from the Torah, the first five books of the Hebrew Bible. Because they did not want to alter the sacred writings, the Massorete scribes noted corrections in the margins.

Fixing the errors and faults in a manuscript is called **amending.** The modern profession of amending ancient texts requires special skills and training. These scholars, who must be familiar with many different ancient scripts, study as many copies of the same ancient manuscript as possible. After careful examination and historical research, experts amend the text to the best of their knowledge.

Copying the Hebrew Bible

A good example of amendation is the Hebrew Bible, which is also known as the Old Testament. The Hebrew Bible gives an early history of the ancient Hebrew people—who lived in what are now Israel and Jordan—and has been sacred to the Jews for hundreds of years. The text was written during the eleventh century B.C., but Hebrew scholars did not decide which sections of the Bible to hold as sacred until the second century A.D.

The experts' indecision resulted from the condition of the original text, which seemed to contain many errors. For about 500 years, Hebrew scholars were reluctant to tamper with the holy writing. Then, in the seventh century A.D., a group of Hebrew scholars called Massoretes—meaning "men of tradition"—began to amend the text of the Hebrew Bible.

As the Massoretes proceeded, they discovered that the original manuscript contained almost 1,500 verses with possible errors. These scholars did not change the sacred writings but instead noted in the margins what they believed were the correct words.

A modern scribe uses traditional methods to create a megillah, a scroll containing the biblical Book of Esther, which is read aloud during the Jewish holiday of Purim.

The errors occurred despite concentrated efforts by Hebrew scribes. These copiers prepared duplicates of the Hebrew Bible according to a complicated set of instructions that had to be followed carefully. This was especially important in making Torahs, which contained the first five books of the Hebrew Bible and were used in synagogues.

The instructions described exactly what materials scribes should write on, the dimensions of the sheets and how they should be fastened together, and how to make the proper ink. The directions also showed scribes how to prepare the surface for writing and how many columns could be put on each scroll. Scribes were even told the correct number of letters for each line of text.

Religious Orders

During the Middle Ages (A.D. 400 to A.D. 1500), many Christian monks in Europe were scribes who copied and collected important works in their libraries. Most monks lived in monasteries—small Christian communities—that devoted their lives to God and to the service of others. The Benedictine monastic order considered copying nearly as important as praying. Benedictine monks spent their days praying, working in the fields, and copying manuscripts.

The Benedictine abbey of Mont St. Michel perches atop a rocky islet along the coast of northwestern France. During the Middle Ages (A.D. 400 to A.D. 1500), the monks of many Christian religious orders dedicated their lives to copying manuscripts.

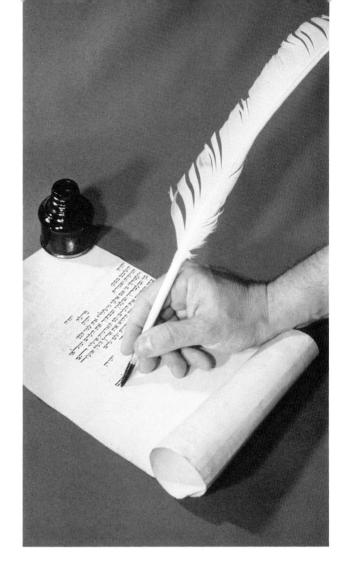

A modern scribe uses a quill pen and ink to write Hebrew characters. These pens were widely used by European scribes of the Middle Ages, who could easily manipulate the hard quill tips to create intricate lettering and detailed designs.

Copying was done mostly on parchment and vellum in a special writing room called a scriptorium. Scribes wrote with hard, pointed quill pens, which were made from feathers. The monks' work was highly specialized. One group produced the parchment, while another did the copying. Other monks might decorate the manuscripts or bind the finished pages into books.

At times, good-quality parchment was scarce, and the monks erased old texts to write new manuscripts. Many prayer books and religious texts were written in bold, black ink over the faded writing of an ancient author. Such writing materials are called palimpsests.

To paleographers, the ancient texts are usually more valuable than the newer writings. To read the early texts, these experts place palimpsests under special ultraviolet and infrared lights, which reveal the original writing. Using this method, the works of many ancient authors, lawyers, and teachers have been recovered.

This manuscript illustration depicts a monastic scribe from the Middle Ages. Although the image portrays the monk writing in a bound book, scribes usually worked on loose sheets that were folded later.

Illuminated Manuscripts

Manuscripts prepared by monks and by other European scribes of the Middle Ages are especially famous for their brilliant, detailed illustrations. One type of text illustration is called **illumination** because the resulting picture looks as if it was lit from the inside.

Different countries of Europe—particularly England, Ireland, France, and Italy—developed their own distinctive styles of illumination. But each of these unique styles incorporated basic elements of decoration, including animals and human figures, branches with leaves or berries, geometric designs, and ornamental letters. Scribes also drew designs called plaits, which looked like braids, as well as scrollwork (curved lines with curled ends).

An illuminated letter decorates a page from the Worms Bible, which was penned in Germany in about 1148. A special art form, illumination features elaborate details and vivid colors. To make the image appear as though it was lit from behind, artists and scribes layered the colors. The darker hues went on first, and lighter tints were applied last.

ALCUIN'S STANDARDS

During the early part of the Middle Ages (A.D. 400 to A.D. 1500), many residents of western Europe could not read or write. The most educated people were generally Christian monks, who copied manuscripts and kept them in monastic libraries. But the monks' writing methods were often chaotic. Words and sentences, for example, sometimes ran together and changed the meaning of phrases and passages.

King Charlemagne—who ruled much of western Europe during the A.D. 700s—was concerned about education and about the preservation of ancient writings. In A.D. 781, he invited Alcuin, an Anglo-Saxon scholar and clergyman, to develop a new script to be used throughout the realm. Called Carolingian minuscule, this writing system became the standard form in western Europe.

Alcuin's new system included uniform spelling and punctuation. For the first time, phrases were divided into sentences, capital letters began sentences, and spaces had to be placed between words. Alcuin's rules also separated text into paragraphs. Carolingian minuscule later became the model for printed type, and the rules of this script remain the standard for writing in modern times.

Alcuin, an eighth-century Anglo-Saxon scholar, developed a system of writing called Carolingian minuscule, which included standards for how text should appear on a page. These standards included dividing the text into sentences and paragraphs.

A cross appears within the carpet pattern of this page from the Lindisfarne Gospels, a late seventh-century illuminated manuscript produced in northeastern England by the Anglo-Saxon monastic scribe Eadfrith.

One of the first steps in illuminating a manuscript was to score the page with guide rules and make detailed sketches. Scribes applied color to the designs in a specific order. The first layer was gold paint, which the artist accented with gold leaf (a thin sheet of the precious metal). The palest colors of paint, such as light hues of pink, green, and blue, were applied next, followed by middle and then darker tints. Scribes then outlined some details with black pen and carefully finished the painting with fine hairline accents of white. These illustrations contained not only intricate designs but also detailed portrayals of European life in the Middle Ages.

THE SURVIVAL OF ANCIENT LITERATURE

The earliest texts were written mainly on materials that crumbled over time. Monks and scribes made copies on more durable materials. As a result, many works survived until the invention of printing, which made mass production of manuscripts possible. Archaeologists have also found writings on stone and clay, that might otherwise have been lost forever.

The Book of the Dead

Archaeological discoveries of ancient texts in Egypt have led to a better understanding of the funeral rites of this early civilization. The Egyptians strongly believed in the afterlife (an existence after death) and spent a great deal of time preparing for death and burial. For example, Egyptians preserved the bodies of the dead for the next life through a process called mummification, which prevented the corpse from decaying.

In the graves, Egyptians buried clothing, food, jewelry, and other objects to help the dead during their journey to the afterlife. Family members also left texts containing instructions on how to proceed to the next world. Collectively, these texts became known as the Book of the Dead.

The Book of the Dead came in many versions, and different texts contained various chapters. Some books were composed of prayers, spells, and burial ceremonies. Other books described the afterlife, detailing the dangers of the next world. Before death, wealthy Egyptians sometimes hired a scribe to write a personalized prediction of their existence in the afterlife.

Egyptian artists often decorated the walls of tombs with passages from the Book of the Dead and accompanied them with illustrations. The illustrations, which were often colorful and detailed, depicted many scenes, including family members carrying funeral objects and the deceased living in heavenly fields. Archaeologists have learned much about the burial practices and religious beliefs of the ancient Egyptians by studying these elaborate paintings.

Surrounded by hieroglyphics, a scene from **The Papyrus of Ani—an Egyptian Book of the Dead—***portrays the weighing of the soul* (center).

The Dead Sea Scrolls

In 1947 nomadic herders called Bedouin found the first of a group of religious writings known as the Dead Sea Scrolls in a cave in Khirbat Qumran. This Middle Eastern site is located on the northwestern shore of the Dead Sea in the region between Israel and Jordan called the West Bank. After the first discovery, Bedouin and archaeologists searched other caves in the region. By the early 1950s, these groups had located 10 more caves containing ancient writings.

The Dead Sea Scrolls consist of more than 800 complete or nearly complete manuscripts, most of which are written in Hebrew and Aramaic—two languages that originated in the Middle East. Excavators also uncovered hundreds of thousands of manuscript fragments

Discovered in these caves near Khirbat Qumran in the West Bank— a region between Israel and Jordan—the Dead Sea Scrolls consist of hundreds of ancient religious documents. Archaeologists believe the writings were stored in the caves by the Essenes, a Jewish religious community that lived nearby.

Although the Essenes wrote mostly on papyrus or leather, archaeologists have also discovered writings on ostraca.

from about 600 other documents. Most of the Dead Sea Scrolls were written on leather or papyrus, and some date to as early as 200 B.C. Many scholars believe that these writings were compiled by the Essenes, a Jewish group that lived in a monastery near the caves.

The Dead Sea Scrolls include almost all 24 books of the Old Testament Bible. Many of the books are almost intact. Excavators also found fragments of the Septuagint, the oldest known Greek translation of the Old Testament. In addition to these religious documents, the Dead Sea Scrolls include the original writings of the Essenes. Some manuscripts describe how this group was organized, and others contain the rules for daily life in the community. These documents provide a clear picture of how the Essenes lived more than 2,000 years ago.

For many years, only a select group of scholars studied the Dead Sea Scrolls. These experts limited access by other scholars to translations and interpretations of the writings. In 1991, however, the Huntington Library in San Marino, California, opened its complete photographic record of the Dead Sea Scrolls to the public. Since that time, the scrolls have been published, and hundreds of experts have been examining the documents. Most scholars are searching for new information about the history of Judaism and Christianity—two religions that began in the area that is now Israel and Jordan.

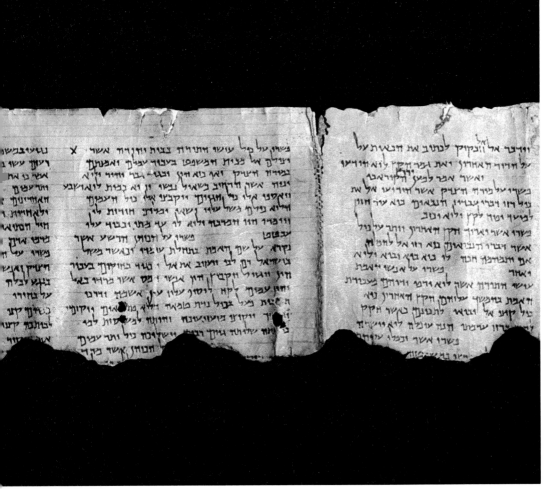

These pages from the Dead Sea Scrolls show grids that guided the scribes.

The Codex Sinaiticus

The earliest surviving Greek book is the Codex Sinaiticus, a Christian Bible containing both the Old Testament and the New Testament, which describes the life of Jesus and his apostles. Dating to the fourth-century A.D., the Greek manuscript was written on about 730 vellum pages, of which only 390 have survived.

In 1844 the German biblical scholar Constantine von Tischendorf found the Codex Sinaiticus at St. Catherine's Monastery near the slopes of Mount Sinai in Egypt. According to Tischendorf, the monks of the monastery were just about to burn the book as fuel when he saved it from destruction. Tischendorf asked the monks to let him take the manuscript back to Germany. The monks decided to keep the codex but gave him 43 of its pages.

Fifteen years later, Tischendorf returned to the monastery and persuaded the monks to loan him the rest of the manuscript. Although he gave the monks a letter saying that he would return the borrowed codex after he finished studying it, Tischendorf instead presented it to the czar of Russia. In 1933 the Soviet Union sold its portion of the Codex Sinaiticus to the British Museum. The other 43-page section of this important manuscript is on display in the University Library of Leipzig in Germany.

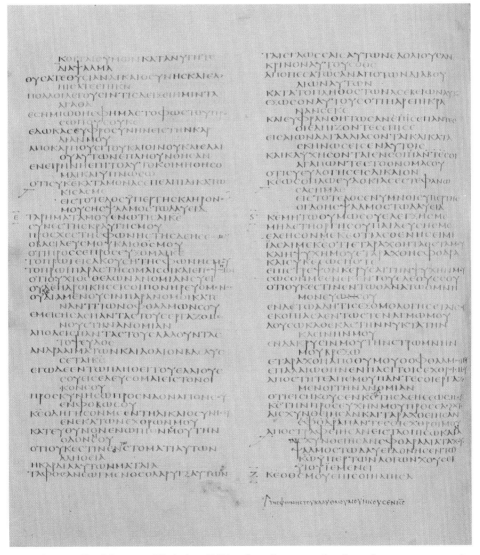

The Codex Sinaiticus, a Christian Bible that dates to the fourth century A.D., is the oldest surviving Greek book.

The Book of Kells

Experts consider the *Book of Kells* to be one of the world's most beautiful manuscripts. This illuminated manuscript, which was written in Latin on fine parchment, contains the Gospels—the first four books of the New Testament—as well as other Christian writings.

The *Book of Kells* was produced by monastic scribes in Ireland between the mid-700s and the early 800s A.D. Scholars believe that many different scribes and artists worked on this manuscript over the decades. Inspired by works from Rome, Egypt, the Middle East, and eastern Asia, the skilled Irish artisans created their own unique artistic style.

For example, the Irish scribes borrowed a rounded form of handwriting called uncial from the Romans. Unlike the Romans, however, the Irish carefully spaced and deliberately formed each individual uncial letter. Although beautifully written, the text itself is full of omissions and mistakes.

Artists took much greater care with the drawings in the *Book of*

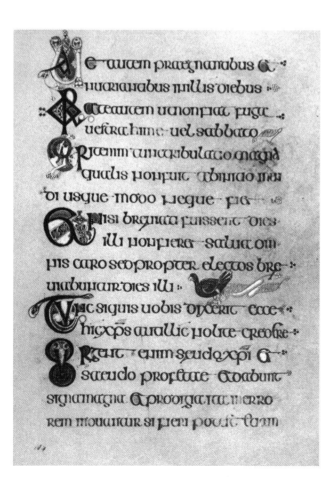

Irish monastic scribes used Insular—an adaptation of the Roman script uncial—to inscribe the Book of Kells, *a copy of the Christian Gospels. The Insular style can be identified by the wedge-shaped tips of some letters.*

An illumination from the Book of Kells *reveals brilliant gold leaf topped with stunning hues of blue, red, and green. Nearly every page of the* Book of Kells *displays elaborate decorations.*

Kells. The monks used fine quill pens dipped in brilliant hues of blue, yellow, green, red, and black to create intricate designs. To fix the colors on the page and to prevent colors from mixing, scribes often coated the design with a thin layer of egg white and water or with gelatin glue. This method also helped to add depth to the drawings.

The illustrated subjects in the *Book of Kells* include portraits of Jesus and his followers, as well as scenes from the Gospels. Another recurring image is the symbol of the cross worked into designs that experts call carpet pages because they resemble Oriental rugs. But the most famous illuminations in the *Book of Kells* are the initial, or first, letters of passages or chapters. Sometimes taking up an entire page, these intricately patterned letters are often intertwined with images of people and animals.

Some parts of the *Book of Kells* were never finished. These sections have allowed scholars to study different stages in the process of

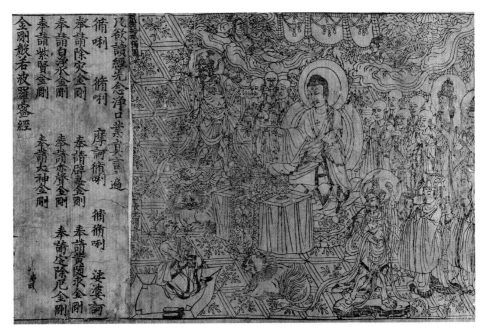

The oldest surviving printed manuscript is the **Diamond Sutra, which was made in China in** A.D. **868. Each of the work's seven sheets was printed by inking a carved block of wood and pressing the block onto paper to produce an image.**

illumination. The *Book of Kells* is now displayed in the library at Trinity College in Dublin, Ireland.

The Invention of Printing

In A.D. 770, the Japanese invented block printing, the earliest form of printing. With this method, artists carved a series of raised characters on wooden blocks, inked the characters, and pressed the inked blocks onto paper.

A Chinese printer made the first movable type in A.D. 1045, by making a separate piece of clay type for each character. In this way, the characters could be arranged in any order. But the use of movable type did not develop any further in China because the Chinese language has thousands of characters—too many for practical use.

Until the fourteenth century, when the use of block printing spread westward, Europeans were still copying manuscripts by hand. At the same time, a period of intensive intellectual and artistic activity known as the Renaissance was sweeping through Europe. This desire for learning created a demand for books that hand copying and block printing could not meet.

To solve this problem, a German printer named Johannes Gutenberg invented a mold that produced separate, uniformly shaped letters of the Roman alphabet, in which

German and other European languages are written. Each piece of type represented one letter, and the pieces could be easily arranged in any order.

By 1440 Gutenberg was using a printing press—made from a machine that originally pressed grapes—to produce multiple copies of a manuscript. He assembled the movable type into a page format, inked the type, placed paper on top of the type, and turned a screw that pressed the paper and type tightly together. This process was repeated for each page of a manuscript.

The invention of printing helped to preserve the content of many ancient texts. When thousands of copies of a work exist, the chances are small that all duplicates will be lost or destroyed. Today, the writings of ancient authors appear in many different languages in millions of books around the world. Books are now even recorded on audio tape or stored on computer disks. For these reasons, even if the original work of an early author or scribe cannot exist forever, the ideas and events of ancient times will be preserved.

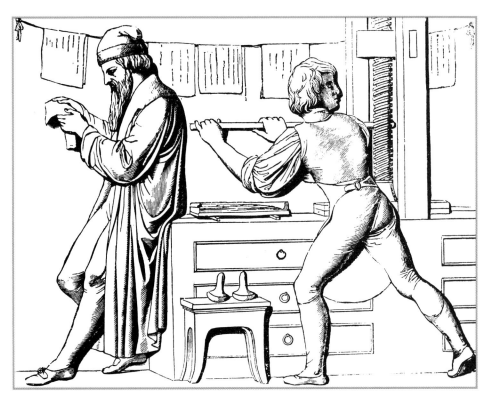

Johannes Gutenberg (left) examines a printed sheet as it comes off the press. The German printer's invention of movable type—individual letters cast from molds that could be arranged in any order—enabled him to produce many copies of a wide variety of writings.

PRONUNCIATION GUIDE

Aborigine (aab-uh-RIHJ-uh-nee)

Aramaic (aar-uh-MAY-ihk)

Bedouin (BED-uh-wuhn)

Codex Sinaiticus (KOH-deks sy-NY-tih-kuhs)

cuneiform (kyoo-NEE-uh-form)

Essene (ihs-EEN)

Gutenberg (GOO-tuhn-berk)

hieroglyphic (hy-ihr-uh-GLIHF-ihk)

Khirbat Qumran (kihr-baht koom-RAHN)

Massorete (MAS-uh-reet)

Maya (MY-uh)

mnemonic (nih-MAHN-ihk)

ostraca (AHS-truh-kuh)

papyrus (puh-PY-ruhs)

quipu (KEE-poo)

quire (KWY-uhr)

Septuagint (sep-TYOO-uh-juhnt)

Tischendorf (TISH-uhn-dorf)

uncial (UHN-shuhl)

vellum (VEHL-uhm)

Taken in 1898, this photograph shows a Jewish scholar pouring over thousands of manuscript fragments found in Cairo, Egypt. Called the Cairo Geniza, these tenth-century A.D. writings detail many aspects of Jewish life.

GLOSSARY

alphabet: a series of symbols used to write a language.

amending: the science of correcting an ancient text that was not copied perfectly and contains errors.

archaeologist: a scientist who studies the material remains of past human life.

codex: a group of wax tablets fastened together like a book. The codex was the forerunner to the modern book.

cuneiform: a writing system consisting of wedge-shaped characters. The ancient Sumerians invented cuneiform for record keeping.

excavate: to dig out and remove objects from an archaeological site.

hieroglyphics: a system of writing in which picture-characters represent objects, ideas, or sounds. Hieroglyphics were used by the ancient Egyptians and the ancient Maya.

ideogram: a picture or a symbol that represents an idea rather than a sound.

illumination: the art of illustrating a manuscript with elaborate designs or miniature pictures. Using the illumination technique, artists layer colors to make the illustrations look like they are lit from behind.

logograph: a symbol that represents a word.

mnemonic: a technique or device used to trigger a person's memory.

ostraca: pieces of pottery used as writing material.

papyrus: sheets of writing material made from the stems of the papyrus plant, which grew along Egypt's Nile River.

parchment: writing material made from the skins of sheep, goats, or cows. Parchment, which has the consistency of a thin sheet of cardboard, provides a smooth writing surface.

pictograph: an ancient drawing that stood for an object or an action.

prehistory: the period of time before the existence of written history.

rebus writing: a visual representation of syllables or entire words by pictures of objects or by symbols whose names sound like the intended words or intended syllables.

scroll: a long sheet of writing material rolled into the shape of a tube.

stylus: a sharp writing instrument used to inscribe characters onto wax or clay tablets.

vellum: a fine grade of parchment made from the skins of calves or kids (young goats).

INDEX

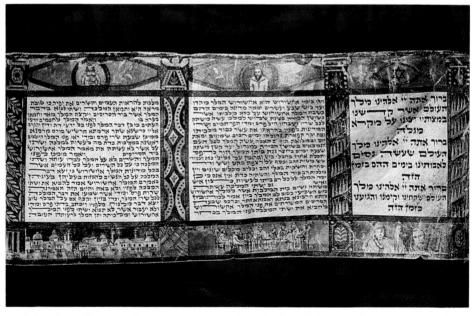

This brightly illustrated megillah was crafted in Israel during the early twentieth century.

A visitor to the Temple of Karnak in Egypt is dwarfed by the site's enormous hieroglyphic-covered pillars.

Photo Acknowledgments

Z. Radovan, Jerusalem, pp. 2, 33 (bottom), 37 (top), 51, 53; French Government Tourist Office, p. 7; Independent Picture Service, pp. 8, 13, 20 (bottom), 22 (bottom), 25, 27, 28, 35 (bottom), 43, 45, 47, 50, 52, 62; Government Tourist Department Tahiti, p. 9; Nigel Harvey, p. 10 (top); Trustees of the British Museum, pp. 10 (bottom), 22 (top), 31, 57, 59, 60; Australian Information Service, p. 11; Laura Westlund, p. 12; Phoebe A. Hearst Museum of Anthropology, University of California at Berkeley, p. 14; Ashmolean Museum, Oxford, 1910.211 ISO 894 DMG 278, p. 15 (top); Kenichi Tazawa, p. 15 (bottom); The Alphabet Makers, courtesy Museum of the Alphabet, pp. 16, 24, 29, 40, 46, 48, 49, 56; Dr. Steven Derfler, pp. 19, 33 (top); University of Minnesota College of Architecture and Landscape Architecture, pp. 21 (top), 32, 36; Library of Congress, pp. 17, 21, 67; Cultural and Tourism Office of the Turkish Embassy, p. 23; Andrew Beswick, p. 26; The Metropolitan Museum of Art (30.4.11), p. 34; The Bade Institute, Pacific School of Religion, pp. 35 (top), 61; Skirball Museum, Hebrew Union College, p. 37 (bottom), 70; Jost Amman, The Book of Trades, p. 38; The Edward E. Ayer Collection, The Newberry Library, p. 41; Wisconsin Paper Council, p. 42; Trinity College Library, Cambridge (Ms. R.17.1 f.283v), p. 54; British Library, London, pp. 55, 63, 66; Board of Trinity College, Dublin, pp. 64, 65; The Library of the Jewish Theological Seminary of America, p. 68; Jeanne Conte, p. 71.

Cover photographs: Bob Schlosser (front) and Armenian Library and Museum of America (back).